Civic Skills and Values

Honesty

By Dalton Rains

www.littlebluehousebooks.com

Copyright © 2024 by Little Blue House, Mendota Heights, MN 55120. All rights reserved. No part of this book may be reproduced or utilized in any form or by any means without written permission from the publisher.

Little Blue House is distributed by North Star Editions:
sales@northstareditions.com | 888-417-0195

Produced for Little Blue House by Red Line Editorial.

Photographs ©: Shutterstock Images, cover, 7, 8–9, 10–11, 12, 15, 18–19, 20, 24 (top left), 24 (top right), 24 (bottom left), 24 (bottom right); iStockphoto, 4, 16–17, 23

Library of Congress Control Number: 2022919849

ISBN
978-1-64619-817-7 (hardcover)
978-1-64619-846-7 (paperback)
978-1-64619-902-0 (ebook pdf)
978-1-64619-875-7 (hosted ebook)

Printed in the United States of America
Mankato, MN
082023

About the Author

Dalton Rains writes and edits nonfiction children's books. He lives in Minnesota.

Table of Contents

Telling the Truth **5**

Struggles **13**

Why It Matters **21**

Glossary **24**

Index **24**

Telling the Truth

Honesty means telling the truth.

It means you do not cheat or lie.

Honesty happens at home. You try to do all your chores. But you do not lie if they are not done.

An adult says you can have one cookie.
You do not lie and take more from the jar.

Honesty means everyone can have fun.

You can play a game with your family.

You play by the rules and do not cheat.

Struggles

Sometimes it is hard to be honest.

You might not want to tell the truth.

Mistakes happen a lot, and that is okay.

You might break a vase at home.

You might not want to tell an adult.

Maybe you are not ready for a test at school.

You do not know the answer to a question.

You might want to look at your friend's answer.

It feels bad to make a mistake, but it is important to be honest. You should not cheat or lie.

Why It Matters

Everyone makes mistakes. You can learn from what you did wrong. Then you can do better.

Honesty is important. It helps you, and it helps other people.

Glossary

game

test

jar

vase

Index

A
answer, 16

C
chores, 6

F
family, 10

S
school, 16